SIMPLE
Decorating

MELISSA MICHAELS

HARVEST HOUSE PUBLISHERS
EUGENE, OREGON

Contents

Praise for *Simple Decorating*

"This book is brimming with decorating advice and inspiration you will want to test-drive in your own home after reading just the first few pages. Melissa helped me hone the style that works best for my family and lifestyle, and she shared so many real-life tips for decorating our home!"
— LIZ FOUREZ, founder of LoveGrowsWild.com, author of *A Touch of Farmhouse Charm*

"Sometimes even the most creative people get stuck when it comes to decorating their own home. Melissa is full of simple, easy-to-execute ideas that will get those decorating wheels turning! Her words motivate and nurture, and you'll want to come back to them again and again as you tweak, collect, and arrange your way through the process of making a home you love."
— MARIAN PARSONS, *Miss Mustard Seed* (blog)

What People Are Saying About *Love the Home You Have* and *The Inspired Room*

"Melissa shares how to be content and happy in our home, inspiring our home with the things we love and the people we cherish."
— ANN VOSKAMP, *New York Times* bestselling author of *One Thousand Gifts*

"Melissa Michaels' book *The Inspired Room* is full of smart, practical advice and packed with inspiration to spare. The photos are gorgeous and accompanied by helpful tips and details, and the writing lifts you up and makes you excited to dive into home decor headfirst!"
— SHERRY PETERSIK, *New York Times* bestselling author of *Young House Love*

"Melissa Michaels, how did you get into my every house-obsessed thought?"
— JILL WAAGE, executive editor, *Better Homes and Gardens* Brand

"I just love Melissa's approach to decorating to give yourself time to let the process of decorating happen in your home. Give yourself grace as well and enjoy the process."
— RACHEL DOWD, *Sweet and Simple Home* (blog)

"The ideas and tips Melissa shares can be done by anyone, in any decorating style, and even on the tiniest of budgets."
— DIANE HENKLER, *In My Own Style* (blog)

"Melissa is warm, down-to-earth, and exactly the kind of friend you want to come beside you to help turn your house into a home you can love and use to love others."
— MARY CARVER, author of *Choose Joy*

"Melissa offers the cure to comparison every woman needs: contentment. She'll inspire you to have a home that's not only lovely but also a true reflection of what matters most to you."
— HOLLEY GERTH, author of *You're Already Amazing*

Cover by Nicole Dougherty
Cover image © Irtsya / Shutterstock
Interior design by Faceout Studio, Paul Nielsen

Published in association with William K. Jensen Literary Agency, 119 Bampton Court, Eugene, Oregon 97404.

SIMPLE DECORATING

Copyright © 2016 by Melissa Michaels
Published by Harvest House Publishers
Eugene, Oregon 97402
www.harvesthousepublishers.com

ISBN 978-0-7369-6311-4 (soft cover)
ISBN 978-0-7369-6312-1 (ebook)

Library of Congress Cataloging-in-Publication Data

Names: Michaels, Melissa, author.
Title: Simple decorating / Melissa Michaels.
Description: Eugene, Oregon : Harvest House Publishers, [2016]
Identifiers: LCCN 2016023943 (print) | LCCN 2016024537 (ebook) | ISBN 9780736963114 (pbk.) | ISBN 9780736963121 ()
Subjects: LCSH: Interior decoration. | House furnishings--Psychological aspects.
Classification: LCC NK2115 .M464 2016 (print) | LCC NK2115 (ebook) | DDC 747--dc23
LC record available at https://lccn.loc.gov/2016023943

Printed in China

16 17 18 19 20 21 22 23 24 25 / DS – FO / 10 9 8 7 6 5 4 3 2 1

SIMPLE DECORATING

is for real life—including the chaos of change. This book was created during our move from one home to another. Images from the two houses will give you a chance to see tips, accessories, and furniture in different settings and seasons. So, welcome to these imperfect and real spaces! They offer the decorating lessons I've learned through the years. As you consider ideas for your home, remember that imperfection doesn't have to feel like a limitation—it can be a creative opportunity to make the most of what you have and love.

A PLACE YOU
CAN CALL HOME

Do you ever find yourself in a decorating slump or just plain ol' STUCK? Whether you spend hours drooling over your favorite rooms on Pinterest or feel so frozen you don't even know what to look for, I created this little guide to give you a gentle nudge toward a home you'll love.

Feeling confident in your own style and with your decor choices might take time. It helps to start with the courage to experiment and the inspiration to spark your ideas. If you don't know your style or the mood you're after, you can end up with a hodgepodge of items that individually seemed like good ideas but altogether just don't work. You might have hand-me-downs to sit on, an empty space still waiting for inspiration, or a room full of pieces you love. No matter what your starting point is, if you know how to mix and match elements together, you can make your unique design statement and a home that is exactly how you dream it should be.

The truth I share every day on *The Inspired Room* blog and will express in these pages is that you don't have to start with a dreamy house, nor do you have to spend a fortune to make what you have more beautiful. A magazine or Internet image of a room that catches your eye is often a Photoshop-enhanced presentation of a well-designed corner with curated items all set up for the perfect shot. While a beautiful photo can inspire us and we might even capture magazine cover looks, what really matters in our home is how it feels to be there. A home is a place to dwell. It's a sanctuary that can invite us to be ourselves. Our home should be a comfortable haven, with rooms and spaces we enjoy being in.

Every part of your home can be an authentic reflection of what you love, arranged in a livable, pleasing, and lovable space for your family to gather. So let's explore how you can simply create a beautiful place that you can call home in every sense of the word.

Feeling confident in your own style
and with your decor choices might take time.
It helps to start with the courage to experiment
and the inspiration to spark your ideas.

Signature STYLE

Signature
STYLE

If you pick up a design book or magazine, you will often find that each one represents a specific style, with tips and photo illustrations for how to achieve that look. You may even find quizzes to identify your style or definitions of various looks to choose from. Yet a home is so personal!

While it can be helpful to have terms to describe your signature look, I don't think you actually have to *choose* a style, especially one that has its own label in a book or in the design world. In fact, to have a truly personal style, there has to be something a bit unexpected about it. Something previously undefined. Something that is all you.

You will define your style by *living* it first. Your life experiences and personal preferences should inspire the look and feel of your home. Perhaps like me, your faith and family are priorities. What motivates your decisions, and what passions impact your life? These are elements you can incorporate into your home. No one will share your exact style because there is only one you! Your style will ebb and flow through each changing season of your life, springing from your unique personality and reflecting the joy you find in living. So go ahead and create a style that has no official designer name. Boldly design a look inspired by your life and everything you love. Mix it all up to give your home its own unique flair, creating the perfect space for you to come home to each day!

DESIGN YOUR LIFE FIRST

Make style and decor choices that support the life you have and the one you want. If you have pets or small children, you might pay more attention to the durability of fabrics. If you can't spend much time keeping up your home, make decor choices that are simpler and more forgiving so you can spend less time cleaning. If you hope to travel more, go for low-maintenance options. Your home is *for* you and your family, so always consider how your home can accommodate what you enjoy. A comfortable place to watch movies? Space to cook a delicious meal? An organized craft closet to inspire your hobbies?

Consider the unique personality and needs of you and your family. Do you need an escape, a retreat from busy or stressful days at work? Do you want your home to be a place for community with an open door and gathering spaces for neighbors and friends? Make choices that will shape your home into a place where you get to be yourself.

Think about future goals and needs. In light of where you're headed, is your home a short-term or life-long dwelling? If you will move again in the near future, keep affordability, mobility, and flexibility in mind as you select furniture and styles, while still creating a place you feel comfortable in for the time being. If you are settling in for the long term, what choices might grow with you and your family's needs? What areas of improvement might you invest in more fully?

2 | DISCOVER YOUR STYLE

What do you love? What says "home" when you walk into a room? Discover your style by noticing what tones, colors, shapes, and arrangements you would like your home to model in its own way—in your own way. Descriptive words and inspirational images will help lead the way!

Brainstorm inspiration words. Create a short list of words to express the look you want. Think about who you are, what you like, and how others might describe you. Consider the style of your home's architecture, the surrounding landscape, your favorite books, hobbies, style of clothing, etc. If you don't live alone, list words that describe your family, your spouse. A few of my inspiration words are:

nature, clean	happy, sophisticated	collected, refreshing
airy, light	approachable, relaxed	sea, getaway

Browse images. Consider it an investment and not an indulgence to look at magazines and favorite online sources for photos of rooms you connect with. If you see a style you love, study it and dream up your version of it. The most helpful examples will have at least one aspect in common with your space: room size or layout, style of windows, architectural details, etc. This might spark more ideas for your inspiration word list.

3 | DIY: CRAFT AN INSPIRATION BOARD

Keep your style in mind and in view with an inspiration board for your home or for each room! You can make a virtual one, but consider creating at least one physical board as an exercise in bringing your style to life.

1. Choose a bulletin board. Or find a blank space on a wall you can take over for a season.

2. Gather some inspiration elements. Search your home, magazines, online sources, and even the outdoors for photos or objects that represent what makes your heart sing. Include mementos, scrapbook paper, fabric and paint swatches, fonts, photos, leaves or flowers, and your doodles of lamps, patterns, or furniture arrangements.

3. Arrange and pin the pieces. The pleasure of grouping, overlapping, and rearranging the colors, photos, textures, and ideas becomes a vacation from your usual routine. It can be addicting!

4. Hang the board where it will motivate you. But don't stop there. Continue brainstorming throughout the week. Pull elements down that you grow tired of and put new ones up as you feel inspired. See what works, what clashes, what feeds your vision!

5. Take a photo. This visual reference will keep you focused on your style goals when you are out looking for particular pieces.

4 | CREATE A STYLE WISH LIST

If you have a specific style you like, it's helpful to discover which elements will inspire your own look. Let's say you want a farmhouse-style home. Do some research of designers online or in books to find others who have a similar aesthetic. Dissect their rooms and make a list of elements used in their designs that you could incorporate into your own. Don't be intimidated by price tags or designer brands. Look closely at your favorite designers' rooms, and you'll likely find you can get a similar look for less. Keep your style wish list on hand for when you shop! Your list will help you to have specific pursuits at retail outlets, estate sales, or thrift stores and confirm what you need to weed out.

Include in your list both general references (more antiques, certain colors) and specific elements (iron chandelier, wood trestle table). Once you can translate your style into tangibles, you'll be able to reduce costly and often regrettable random purchases.

5 | CHANGE YOUR STYLE ON A BUDGET

When you think a room feels uninspired and you're tight on funds, consider it an opportunity to be more creative. What can you do for free (or cheap)?

Try something unexpected. Use a stool for an end table, floor pillows for casual extra seating, a hutch as a bookcase, or a wire basket as wall art.

Clear out the unloved. Identify things you don't want or need. You might find stuff tucked away that you could repurpose or sell to save up for something you do want!

Get sentimental. Dig through your postcards and greeting cards. Hang some special notes or current family memories with pushpins or frames.

Look at the overlooked. Missed decorating opportunities are plentiful. Restyle the top of your dresser or end table. What needs to be dealt with, hung up, or put away?

Shake things up. Which items could you move to a new spot? Your usual nightstand lamp could add a homey touch to your kitchen counter. Your wall art in the entry might look wonderful above your bed!

6 | MIX AND MATCH TO GET YOUR LOOK

Style mixing can be a challenging art form. Nobody wants a living room that looks like a yard sale explosion, but staying safe with a matchy-matchy look won't help you shape your signature style. There are ways to mix and match and still have harmony.

SURPRISE

If you have a basic look you are going for, whether that be a particular era or style or basic color scheme, throw in a twist with a piece that doesn't fit the rule so it can stand out as fresh.

SIMPLIFY

When mixing styles, reduce excess clutter that can steal the show and add confusion. Remove unnecessary items off your mantel and tables. Also, simple, neutral wall colors will allow your variety of furniture and accessories to be the focus.

UNITE

A vibrant color on one focal piece brings a pop of personality to a space and creates a visual center. Or one color repeated at least three times in a room (throw pillows, blankets, painted furniture, accessories, and wall colors) can bring a cohesive look to eclectic furniture.

CELEBRATE

Don't force your signature style to fit one label. As long as you can identify it when you see it, feel it, or spot the ideal complement to it, celebrate *your* style.

7 | LET YOUR STORY AND HOME EVOLVE

Creating your home is like writing an ongoing love story. It will keep evolving just as your life and family will. Even though you might be impatient for the end result, remember that the creation process is part of the joy.

+ Use what you have as a starting place and then add one layer at a time.

+ Balance seasons of making changes with seasons of savoring and waiting.

+ Believe that "good enough" really *is* good enough for now.

+ Look for creative solutions, not expensive ones.

+ Let go of a look you used to love in order to make room for your next chapter.

Love your space even during the in-between stage. Let's face it. That stage can be all the time. But that's okay. It's your home, not a showroom. Taking time to hunt for the right pieces and shape your style will ultimately create a more interesting story.

The creation process is part of the joy.

Memorable
MOOD

Memorable MOOD

If you were to pick your favorite escape, the place you'd go to feel refreshed, more fully alive, and in touch with what you most love, where would you go? Close your eyes and picture yourself heading there right now. Perhaps you would head to a local coffeehouse or travel to a charming seaside inn. Maybe your mind travels through time to a place you used to love.

So often the highlight of the year is our vacation, the time we leave our home to go to a different place to rest and rejuvenate. Those getaways from everyday stress and routine are important, but our home is where we spend most of our time. It should be the place that nurtures us and enhances our life, perhaps as much or more than any other place on earth. With some attention to detail and a few extra touches, we can create the mood we long for right where we eat, sleep, live life, and daydream.

You see, the real secret to creating a beautiful space isn't found in just buying the right things or even in having a perfect house to begin with. It's in knowing how to create a place that evokes a feeling. Your home can spark happiness and comfort, joy and peace—whatever you envision as the perfect mood for your escape from the world right there in your own sanctuary.

8 | DRAW INSPIRATION FROM YOUR FAVORITE PLACES

Look to your favorite places to find design elements you can incorporate to create the same mood for your home. When you translate the mood of a special place into ambience for your home, it takes on a richly personal feel.

SPECIAL PLACE	DESIGN POSSIBILITIES
A charming cafe	White walls, marble-and-wood bistro table, chalkboard on the wall
Spas or salons	Dim lighting, natural elements, soothing music
A favorite boutique	Floral wallpaper, crystal chandelier, gold mirrors
A dream island vacation	Coastal elements, lots of natural light, sea-inspired colors
Library nooks	Tall bookshelves, stacks of hardback books, leather chairs
Botanical gardens	Potted plants, nature-inspired colors, botanical prints
European destinations	Antiques, architectural elements, paintings of European settings

SET THE MOOD FOR YOUR SENSES

9

Engaged senses create and awaken good memories, inspire contentment, and transform your surroundings and your mood. Give your senses something to celebrate.

SIGHT

What makes your eyes light up? Create a visual feast that nourishes your sense of home with:

+ furnishings and accessories in different sizes, shapes, and visual weight

+ vibrant, patterned areas balanced with simplicity so your eyes have a place to rest

+ wall colors that flow room to room for visual expansion

+ textures, colors, patterns, shapes, light, and shadow that together create a pleasing big picture

TOUCH

Pay attention to textures as you make decorating decisions and collect:

+ fabrics, accessories, floor coverings, counter materials, or furnishings

+ paired opposites—rough with smooth, shiny with dull, woven with silky

+ natural elements, including wood, stone, and plants for dimension

+ soft additions, such as down-filled pillows, lush blankets, thick natural fiber rugs

+ irresistible touches, such as luxurious sheets, fluffy towels, glass bowls in the kitchen

SMELL

Make a lasting and good impression on guests and your family with a nice scent and a clean home:

+ flower arrangements with subtle scents infuse bedrooms, entries, and bathrooms with beauty

+ signature scents created with candles and natural elements—such as vanilla and nutmeg, cloves for cozy moods, and lemon, jasmine, and orange for vibrant ones—help set a pleasing mood

+ unscented home cleansers will invite even sensitive noses to take deep, happy breaths

SOUND

Create a personalized soundtrack for your family's life with:

+ motivating and mood-setting music for different times of day and activities, such as housework or a dinner party.

+ limited contrasting sounds or repetitious phone beeps and alerts that can agitate

+ access to gentle outside sounds, such as the wind, water features, birds

+ silence during segments of the day

TASTE

Good taste is not just about style, but also about creating home spaces to experience the sense of taste. Try:

+ a soothing area to brew your morning coffee or tea for a day-making ritual

+ food prep stations and dining spaces that suit your style and invite others to savor and stay

+ organized pantries, cupboards, and refrigerators that set the stage to experience good food

HUMOR

Don't leave out your sense of humor! Laughter is always on my family's soundtrack. When a style touch represents our version of comedy, all the better. I'm never opposed to adding a few quirky animals here and there on anything from fabric to accessories in my home! Consider how you might bring your sense of humor to the spirit of your sanctuary.

10 | DISCOVER 8 WAYS TO A HAPPY HOME

1. **Fall in love with one corner.** If your home seems as if it's falling apart, create one happy corner in your study, dining room, or bedroom.

2. **Go back to basic routines.** As you do laundry, cook, or empty the dishwasher, think about how you are improving your home and state of mind. Tidy, putter, relax. Remind yourself of the simple routines, habits, and rhythms that give you peace.

3. **Let home be the centerpiece of your joy.** What are 20 things you look forward to doing in your home? Sort books, create a new display of accessories, rearrange furniture, and place inspiring quotes and photos of people you love around your home. Being optimistic today ensures more joy tomorrow.

4. **Reset the day.** Step away from a stressful house project to change your disposition. Take a walk, sip coffee on the porch, or window-shop to reset the day toward happiness.

5. **Dream.** Imagine the things you would do to your home if time or money were unlimited. Then decide how to make one of those dreams come true soon with a little creativity.

6. **Count those blessings.** Thankfulness for the home you have is an important part of loving life. If you are frustrated by a lack of progress, count the things you love about your home as is.

7. **Treat yourself.** What would make you happy right now? A new pillow in your reading nook chair? A fresh doormat? Pretty, plush towels? A woven basket for your mail? Simple treats can make a big difference in your mood, motivation, and creativity.

8. **Share your home.** Invite friends over to enjoy a space you recently saved from clutter. Gather neighbors on your porch for an impromptu dessert. Hospitality, laughter, and shared moments will remind you of all that makes you happy.

11 | TAKE YOUR CUES FROM THE SEASONS

Even if your corner of the world doesn't show the seasons, create the impression of seasonal freshness and ambience with simple changes around the house.

Enjoy the bounty of the season. Fresh and seasonal fruits and vegetables break up the monotony in your diet and in the colors and shapes you bring into your home. Don't forget to infuse your home with the scents of the season.

Inspire thanksgiving all year. Set a gratitude journal in the entry or living room and invite family and friends to add to it each season.

Capture seasonal scenes. During different times of the year, take photos of your yard, local park, or favorite downtown street. Frame those photos and incorporate them into your decor. Set a summer image by your nightstand when winter stretches on too long.

Keep decorations simple. A seasonal wreath on the front door, a basket of apples on the counter, or a bouquet of freesia can be enough to make a statement.

12 | INSPIRE THE ATMOSPHERE YOU WANT

LIVELY

Your home is where you can come alive and delight in the details. Create an energizing space to boost your mood with just the right mix of elements to inspire and recharge the life you want to live with:

graphic fabric patterns

splashes of vibrant hues

contrasting colors

strikingly shaped accessories

mixed styles of furnishings

bold artwork

displayed collections

energizing music

furniture for people to gather

fresh floral arrangements

dramatic focal points

quirky statement pieces

LOVE
is patient
is kind
does not envy
does not boast
is not proud
does not dishonor others
is not self seeking
is not easily angered
keeps no record of wrongs
does not delight in evil
rejoices with the truth
always protects
always trusts
always hopes
always perseveres
1 Corinthians 13:4-7

SERENE

Do you crave an escape from the noise and frantic pace of the outside world? The choices you make can set a soothing ambience that quiets your mind and inspires rest and relaxation. Your home is where you can be refreshed with:

solid neutral fabrics	fewer pieces
restful colors	clearer surfaces
soft edges	more white space
organic elements	water features
subtle patterns	closed storage
less contrast	simplified design elements

13 | LIGHTEN UP

Your atmosphere will come together when the lighting does. Illuminate your favorite spaces!

+ Walk around your home and note the lights, lamps, dark corners, and the ambience. Then write down where you need lighting for mood, specific tasks, and personality.

+ Let natural daylight into your space with sheer curtains or adjustable shutters and blinds.

+ Use multiple light sources to soften dark corners and cozy up a room instantly.

+ Choose a larger lamp than you might normally consider or enjoy a new creative shape, color, or personality.

+ Add a smaller lamp or two on a console table for charm.

+ Bring in a floor lamp. I prefer small-scale, pharmacy-style metal lamps because they don't take up much room and still add light and personality.

+ Use the right lightbulb for the desired effect. Consider "warm light" bulbs for lamps and "daylight" bulbs for garages or other significant task areas.

+ Mix in two large lamps to enhance conversation areas.

+ Welcome people with gentle lighting in the entryway with wall lamps, sconces, or a small lamp on a table.

+ Consider sconces or the surprise touch of a lamp for ambient light in the kitchen.

+ In the bedroom, overhead lights don't inspire romance or rest, so select lamps that enhance visibility as well as tone, such as nightstand lamps or plug-in style wall sconces for reading.

+ Allow for mood flexibility with dimmer switches in any room!

+ Add special lighting for variety and delight with string lights, hurricane lamps, chandeliers, outdoor lighting features used inside, and candles and more candles.

+ Reflect and maximize light with well-placed mirrors and glass.

14 | LISTEN TO YOUR HOME

Do you ever feel limited by the style of your house, the furniture you've had a long time, or the current trend options? In your heart, you're sure your house would look best with a certain color scheme or style of furniture, but you find yourself stuck by how you think it's "supposed" to be. You might hesitate to try something new because you aren't sure if you can trust your instincts.

What you're sensing in your heart might actually be your house crying out for a fresher color scheme or simplified accessories. An older home might be wishing to retain her charm but with a little more spunk. Of course, a house doesn't literally speak, but consider how you feel in your space to determine what your house actually needs.

What is your house telling you? Try whatever your home is asking for. Worst outcome? You don't like it any better. But best case scenario? You love the new look.

Consider how you feel in your space to determine what your house actually needs.

Beautiful
BACKDROPS

Beautiful
BACKDROPS

Have you ever carefully arranged your furniture and still felt that your room wasn't quite right? Maybe you even piled on the accessories to try to fix it, but something was definitely missing. Or do you sometimes wonder if the best way to decorate a room is to just get a new sofa or perfect chairs? New furniture *is* always fun, but the real secret to creating a beautiful room isn't the right sofa or combination of accessories. It's the *shell* of the room that will make everything else shine!

When an Instagram or Pinterest photo of a beautiful room captures your attention, the backdrop is probably a big part of the attraction. Some of your favorite dream rooms might have charming details such as shiplap walls, endless wood floors, or big windows trimmed in substantial moldings with gorgeous sunlight streaming through.

How wonderful if you have those extra touches or are in a position to add them to your space. But even if real life includes dingy carpet, small windows, or lackluster rooms, there is still hope. There are plenty of simple ways to enhance the architectural impact and that all-important shell for even the humblest of rooms.

15 | CREATE VISUAL FLOW ROOM TO ROOM

Evaluate the visual connection between your spaces. Choose a spot in your home from which to look around 360 degrees. Is there a sense of flow in flooring, colors, furniture, and accents? What stands out in a good or bad way?

Remove objects of distraction. Identify and adjust anything that competes for visual attention. Simplifying your stuff gives your eyes places to rest and frees up the flow between rooms.

Plan your color choices. Select wall colors that offer pleasant contrasts or complements when viewed together. You can achieve a more subtle color flow between adjoining rooms by selecting the same paint for both spaces while adding white paint to lighten the effect in one of the rooms. (Test the ratio until you get a shade you like.) Or use subtly different tones from the same color palette.

Unite with an accent color. Lightly weave an accent color throughout the house in fabrics, curtains, rugs, ceramics, framed art, painted doors, and furniture.

16 | SET THE SCENE WITH PAINT

Walls are the largest backdrop in your home, and their color will make a big impact on the visual flow and the mood of each room. Here are some guides to help you choose perfect-for-you backdrops.

Choose your wall paint colors last. Ideally, let your decor choices evolve and then choose a paint color and finish that will complement rather that dictate your decisions. It's more enjoyable to select furniture you want and then find a complementary paint color than to shop for a sofa and rug based on a predetermined but potentially limiting paint color. You can also enhance and unite furniture and accessories you already have with a complementary backdrop.

Find inspiration for your colors. Look around at nature, books, rugs, paintings, fabrics, accessories, landscape tones...everywhere and anywhere. I usually begin with a color scheme that captures the general mood I want and reflects the surroundings outside and inside my home.

Make it easy. If you become overwhelmed by paint choices, go with a paint brand's recommended palette and then add your personality with slight adjustments or accent colors.

Consider neutrals. If you have good natural light, all white walls can be a great backdrop. Otherwise, the space can feel cold and lifeless. A soft neutral like greige or taupe can be a pleasing way to warm a room.

Don't be intimidated by a dark color. Whether you paint a full room or just one wall, a dark color adds dramatic contrast. Paired with light trim, it can be striking.

Soften harsh lines. If your home has awkward angles, all one tone on the walls, ceiling, and even trim can reduce the sharp lines.

Paint stripes. Bring visual depth and space to a room with stripes on one wall.

Test your choice. Before buying a gallon, paint a large sample section of the color on several walls and observe it for a couple days. The look of a color can change significantly depending on the light.

Make it fun. There are many clever options. Try chalkboard or dry-erase paint in an office, kids' rooms, the pantry (great for shopping lists), or on an interior door.

17 | DEFINE SPACE AND STYLE WITH RUGS

Rugs can make a perfect style statement. They tend to cover a large portion of a room, so selecting the right one for your space is important. With so many choices for sizes, patterns, and colors, these five guiding tips can be helpful.

1. Area rugs can be placed right over existing carpet, with or without a rug pad, to conceal less than ideal flooring, add style, increase comfort, or to help pull together a room.

2. Most rooms with conversation areas benefit from a rug at least 8' x 10' in size. A large room might need a bigger rug or more than one to define multiple functional areas of the space. A 4' x 6' or 5' x 7' can be perfect sizes in an entry or next to a bed.

3. When using a rug to define a space, choose one large enough that it at least fits under the front legs of each furniture piece. This unites the furniture and makes the room feel larger.

4. Runners can brighten up a dark hallway or be a perfect style statement in a kitchen. Be mindful of the rug patterns in adjoining spaces! If you choose a lively-patterned rug for your living room, select a solid, simple stripe or natural weave for an adjoining room or hallway. Too many rugs in a similar pattern or scale can compete for attention and overwhelm a space.

5. If you have neutral and solid upholstery in your space, a patterned rug can be the style setter you need to give your space the wow factor. If a room includes statement patterns and colorful pieces, consider selecting a rug that is textured—think sisal, jute, seagrass—or subtly patterned.

18 | MAXIMIZE YOUR WINDOWS

How you dress your windows can transform a room. Get creative as you consider which hanging preferences, treatment choices, and fabrics bring the best design layers to your home.

Hang curtains tall and wide. Your windows will appear much larger and more light will get in when you hang treatments above and beyond the window frame. I often hang my curtains almost to the ceiling, but only if it works in proportion to the space. If the area of blank wall above your window is too large, hanging the curtains high can dwarf the window.

Use lots of panels. Strive to add enough panels so the width of the fabric is at least double that of the window for fullness.

Place blinds above the window frame. If your window has no molding to interfere with the flow of a roll-up blind, consider attaching the top of the blind directly to the wall above for a graceful, elongated look.

BEFORE

Order blinds to fit. If you have oddly sized windows, order blinds to your specs. If your window is just quite large, you can hang multiple, narrower panels of blinds.

Show off molding with fixed, short rods. Avoid having a distracting line across pretty window molding by placing short, stationary rods only on either side of the window, rather than all the way across. The panels will soften the look while also highlighting the molding.

Add character and function with shutters. Adjustable shutters allow light in and limit visibility from outside, and they are so charming.

Do what works. In our old laundry room, I hung a curtain panel, rolled it up, and tied it in place with twine so it had the appearance of an adjustable shade with the ease of a simple solution.

19 | SELECT CURTAINS FOR EFFECT

+ Heavier fabrics are attractive when they hang to the floor.

+ Lighter fabrics look lovely a bit longer than floor length so they "puddle" and create a soft cloud.

+ Curtains too short? Sew additional fabric onto the base of your curtains for a more dramatic length and hang.

+ A long, single panel might be all you need for a special small window. Draw the curtain panel back with a tie or an ornate rod for a touch of elegance in a bedroom.

20 | EMBELLISH WITH ARCHITECTURAL DETAILS

When it comes to architectural interest, it's all about the details. Think beyond basic builder style and add architectural touches to your home for extra charm and a sense of quality.

+ Add character with wainscoting, which also provides extra support for hooks and other hardware.

+ Install shiplap or tongue-and-groove paneling vertically or horizontally on walls (ceilings too) for a grand impression.

+ Use strips of molding to make current baseboards more substantial, to create your own crown molding at the ceiling line, and to enhance cupboard, cabinet, or room doors.

+ Place finials on your curtain rods for extra eye candy.

+ Upgrade hardware to transform spaces. Consider new door handles, drawer pulls, switch plates, or hooks.

+ Refresh tired cabinets by adhering a layer of veneer paneling, such as beadboard or strips of molding or even bamboo, to create dimension and personality.

+ Remove kitchen or hutch cupboard doors to create open shelving and a significant but easy "architectural" change.

21 | DIY: DESIGN A PERSONALIZED MAP WALL

The map wall I created attracted a lot of interest and questions on my blog, but I must confess that my first attempt was a big fail. Often the best personal touches to a home have a story behind them! I initially tried to put up the maps with wallpaper paste, which did not allow for me to adjust the pieces as I went. I ended up tearing them down and starting over...and finishing this easy way.

1. Select heavy sheets of wrapping paper. Choose maps that represent places you have traveled to, lands you hope to visit someday, or countries where your family originates from. Or select other patterns that inspire you! Make it a meaningful display.

2. Hang the paper with pushpins. Choose pins that suit your decor: regular pins or those with flat or decorative heads. Make sure they are sturdy. Pins are an especially great option for rentals and temporary fixes!

3. Overlap the paper slightly as needed.

4. Wrap them around a corner for added dimension.

*Often the best personal touches
to a home have a story behind them!*

Simplified
SPACES

Simplified
SPACES

Let's face it. Life can be hectic at times. Our days are busy and schedules are complicated, but designing our home or living in it shouldn't cause additional pressure. To combat the stress of the outside world and to make our home a refreshing escape, our design choices can reflect intentional order and simplicity.

Perfection can bring its own anxieties, so instead of endeavoring to create a perfect home, focus on the basics of what really matters to you. Create a backdrop where you can relax, feel at peace, and just be yourself.

There are many simple techniques you can use to streamline your style and pull together what you love. A home doesn't have to be complicated to be beautiful. Just as finding a place for everything and putting everything in its place will bring order to a cluttered room; simplifying your color scheme, your furniture, or your accessories can bring cohesion to your style and less stress to the process.

Focus on simple steps and improvements that will make a significant impact on how you live. The way you set up your home can make you feel either disorganized or inspired. A simplified space and ongoing, intentional style decisions will make the most of what you have and create a haven you'll enjoy.

Let's explore ways to simplify and beautify our home!

22 | DESIGNATE A PURPOSE FOR A ROOM

Approach the decor of a room with intention. Evaluate its purpose and then how to serve that purpose with its furniture and flow. If you get stuck, empty the space and start re-envisioning it with your needs in mind. Forget how the room was labeled in the floor plans. What do *you* want and need this room to be? For example, if your family never uses your dining room, and you're in desperate need of a homeschooling space or a home office, then look at that dining area with new eyes. Once you know the purpose of a room, a new plan will evolve, and a better use of your home will too.

What kind of space will add joy to your life and more life to your home? To get your creative juices flowing, here are some possible rooms you might be in need of:

study room	craft or sewing area
library	sitting room
dining nook	media room
home office	game room
family room	workout space
play area	storage area
writing room	walk-in closet

23 | INSPIRE YOUR ROOMS, INSPIRE YOUR LIFE

Inspired rooms don't have to be complicated or expensive to pull together. Keep it simple! If you want to live authentically, give yourself permission to eliminate the stress of furnishing your home according to style trends or your own expectations. Enjoy simplicity and see how your home will inspire you. Wander through these three easy room refreshes. Do something simple this week to renew one of your rooms.

BEDROOM

Use unexpected furniture. Maybe mix up nightstands by using a dresser for one and a small bookshelf as the other. This will help create a collected feel when combined with a traditional piece.

Layer a fluffy duvet and a mix of pillows. Atop of a cozy duvet, a variety of throw pillows will add dimension and a touch of pure luxury.

Sprinkle the personal throughout. It's your bedroom, so make it personal! Bring in accessories, books, and framed art and photos that speak to your heart and life's journey.

LIVING ROOM

Revive saggy cushions. **Add foam pieces or other stuffing to zippered cushions. If they are sewn, then release part of the seam, fill, then re-stitch. They will look and feel much better.**

Brighten your throw pillows. **Buy or make new pillow coverings that add a color or pattern to your living or family room. For little or no money, you have a big payoff in personality.**

Add flair to your floor. **A new rug or one swapped out from another room will instantly connect the room elements in a new way. Shift toward a different depth of color tone or from a flat rug to one highly textured for even more of a change.**

KITCHEN

Keep the sink clear. This one habit will make your space feel lighter and smell better, and it will welcome you back with cheer for the next mealtime.

Display your cookbook collection. Add colorful bookends—or kitchenware items as your bookends. This visual gathering will inspire a shelf or nook...and you!

Note to self: Create a garden. Bring warmth to your functional spaces. A memo board with uplifting notes and a kitchen garden of herbs are signs of a nurtured life.

24 | THINK IN THREES

See how the rule of three can give you the starting place you've been looking for.

FURNITURE

+ Have the pieces fill no more than two-thirds of your room.

+ Choose a coffee table that is approximately two-thirds as wide as your sofa.

+ A zone that has three pieces of furniture will be visually appealing.

WALL ACCESSORIES

+ Hang artwork or mirrors that are about two-thirds the width of whatever is below them.

+ Create an attractive gallery wall by envisioning a grid on the wall of three rows of three equally sized squares. The center square is your focal point. Hang various sizes of art at each of the intersecting corners.

COLOR

+ An easy interior design equation for your color palette is 60-30-10. The main room color should cover about 60 percent of the room, the secondary color should make up 30 percent, and the accent color is the remaining 10 percent.

+ Using a color three times in fabrics, backdrop elements, or accessory displays creates a cohesive feel in a room.

TEXTURE

+ Every room should have at least three varying textures to bring interest to the space.

+ If your tablescape or shelf surface is lacking substance, cluster objects made of three different textures for display. Consider glass, shells, and a candle. Or wood, stone, and a shiny metal.

25 | UNITE A ROOM WITH REPETITION

Repeated elements unite even the most eclectic rooms.

+ A pair of matching lamps or pillows offer symmetry.

+ Repetition of similar frames on the wall present a soothing backdrop.

+ Numerous white areas will tie together a room full of varied color and pattern.

+ Furniture pieces with a shared fabric pattern or color combination feel intentional.

+ Multiple accessories of a common material, such as glass, lead the eyes around a room.

+ Repeated visual weight provides balance. If you have a large window on one side of the room, counter it with a piece of furniture of similar visual significance on the other side.

26 | INVENT MINI DESTINATIONS

Shaping destinations in your home is a simple way to begin the process of creating the home you dream of. Break each room into several mini areas by defining a purpose for each. Special destinations within the home offer a sense of peace and invitation for you and guests. What kind of destination could transform an underused or cluttered space into a peaceful, purposeful corner?

MINI DESTINATIONS

coffee station	homework zone
reading corner	music area
sewing nook	command center

Mini destinations work well throughout your home, including the kitchen, garage, and outdoor spaces. Once you identify the purpose for your destination, you can create it in a day or an afternoon as you:

+ Clear clutter.

+ Evaluate any problems, such as a lack of light or lack of storage.

+ Introduce solutions that add beauty, not clutter.

+ Choose furniture pieces that suit the size of the space.

+ Assign only one corner or room as a particular kind of station, at least initially.

27 | REARRANGE FOR A WHOLE NEW LOOK

Are you bored with your space? Rather than shopping for all new furniture to change your look, recharge your energy and vision for your home by hunting for treasures around your house to rearrange what you have. The secret to successfully reimagining a space is to be willing to *set aside what is expected* or what you are *used to using* in other rooms of the house in order to try something new.

How could a corner of your home be used more effectively? What would inspire you to enjoy this space more in this season? Try a new furniture arrangement, a fresh color combination, different accessories, or an entirely new purpose for a space!

28 | SHAKE IT UP WITH UNEXPECTED FURNITURE

Chances are that most people have a sofa, coffee table, and chair in their living room. But why not think outside the box to find unique functional pieces that can add more charm and personality?

Here are some pieces you might have or can find in secondhand stores. How could any of these pieces be brought in to your room and repurposed or restyled to be used a functional way? Mix and match to create something new or assign an old piece a new function:

vintage sewing table	dresser
garden stool	window frame
antique secretary desk	potting table
picnic basket	steamer trunk
bar cart	leather suitcase or briefcase
hutch from a china cabinet	school desk
round metal tray	vintage ladder
buffet cabinet	wood chair
milk crate	large wood cable spool
vintage door	woven baskets

Don't forget a signature piece! Enhance a room by adding a signature piece of furniture. This is an item that—because of its color, shape, style, size, element of surprise, or striking presence—offers a wow factor. Multiple signature pieces in a room will make you and guests dizzy, but one well-chosen piece will draw the eye, spark conversation, and infuse your space with energy.

29 | EVERYTHING NEEDS A HOME

The secret to an orderly home is to ruthlessly declutter what you don't use or love and efficiently contain the things you do. Solutions can involve detailed storage systems, but sometimes they are the most simple of solutions, such as a tray, a basket, or a small box. How you organize isn't as important as the visual impact and function of what you have. Your home will be more beautiful when everything has a home and everything is in its place! Find systems and containers that reflect your personality, suit your style, and make your home more efficient.

EVERYDAY ITEM	SIMPLE STORAGE SOLUTION
Earrings, bracelets, and rings	Dipping bowls or small compartments in a drawer
Extra throw blankets	Leaning, decorative ladder or basket
Cleaning supplies	Over-the-door shoe organizer
Paper keepsakes	Labeled binders or lidded box
Vitamins and medications	Lazy Susan in a cupboard
Wayward office supplies	Shallow drawers or tiered organizer
Reusable grocery bags	Designated hooks in the pantry or entry
Kitchen dish towel	Self-adhesive hook on the side of a cabinet
Gift wrap supplies	Under-the-bed boxes
Bathroom toiletries	Rolling cart

Your home will be more beautiful when everything has a home and everything is in its place!

Creative
CONCEALMENTS

Creative
CONCEALMENTS

So, your room isn't perfect? Your windows are too small or your fire-place is off center. Maybe your room is awkwardly shaped, or you have too many doorways. Maybe your ceilings are low or too high. Who was the brilliant one who put the air conditioner in the middle of the wall or tiled that niche with the ugliest selection imaginable? And for the love of all things, why are there no closets in this house?

Welcome to the club. Most of us have imperfect spaces.

Most of us live in a home designed by or for someone else, so we need the freedom to redesign it to suit our needs. We won't feel more comfortable in our home by avoiding the glaring things we don't like or trying to fit our worldly belongings into someone else's limited version of space. We can make this house our home and love living in it!

Easier said than done, right?

Fortunately, home improvement doesn't always require a remodel. There are plenty of ways to creatively conceal awkward features and enhance the visual impact and function of each room. A good starting goal is to challenge yourself to make things *better than they were*. That takes the pressure off, doesn't it? But don't limit your creative potential. You have the power to take that room from "What were they thinking?" to "I can't even believe this is the same room!"

30 | DIRECT THE EYE WITH FOCAL POINTS

Does your room have a visually impactful focal point? In a good way? The focal point of a room should never be something unattractive. If you can't look away from that weirdly sized window or the world's most hideous built-in, then your job is to creatively update or disguise the feature you don't like or create a new focal point that says, "LOOK HERE!" to direct eyes toward a feature you do love.

Our living room had a fireplace we didn't love. The placement was off balance, and the stone and grout had a distracting pink hue. Every time we entered the space, it conflicted with the look we wanted. It incorrectly defined our style.

Without a remodel, we were able to minimize the design woes of the fireplace. We painted the stones a soft gray to better blend in with our color scheme. Then we simply rearranged the furniture away from the fireplace and toward the view outside a large window. Our troublesome stone structure became a secondary feature in the background, and the lovely, outdoor view became the room's focal point.

How can you redirect the line of sight in a room that currently has a less than lovely focal point?

AFTER

BEFORE

31 | HIDE DISTRACTIONS WITH EVERYDAY CONCEALERS

What feature of your home seems worn or awkward and in need of a creative concealment?

CHALLENGE	EVERYDAY CONCEALER
Chaotic, open storage area?	Hang a curtain.
Tired kitchen cupboards?	Paint the fronts or add new doors to the original cabinet boxes.
Ugly cords?	Hide them behind plants and baskets.
Wimpy, worn baseboards?	Paint them to match the walls.
Sloping floor?	Put taller pieces of furniture on the low side for visual balance.

More solutions to get your ideas flowing!

+ Rugs layered or rearranged can hide stained or worn wood or carpeted floors.

+ Fabric panels or hung rectangular tablecloths can enclose basement laundry areas or create makeshift closets.

+ Framed paintings, clocks, or rustic baskets can hide wall imperfections.

+ A simple coat of paint or stain refreshes unsightly furniture.

+ Potted vines, lattice panels, or trellises create private outdoor spaces and block unsightly views.

+ Paint unites mismatched pieces—or different colors can make similar pieces eclectic.

+ Charming shutters, blinds, or stained glass can conceal less than lovely views.

+ Faux board-and-batten or tin ceiling tiles add non-permanent architectural detail.

+ Old doors or a curtain hung behind a bed can give the illusion of a headboard.

+ Glaze or paint applied in varied brushstrokes creates a patina and hides uneven plaster or other wall flaws. Layer a couple colors for more distraction.

+ Outdoor light fixtures used indoors are strong focal points to detract from in-process areas.

+ Chalkboard paint can give fun life and versatility to flawed or ugly doors.

32 | SELECT DECOR-FRIENDLY STORAGE SOLUTIONS

We all have "stuff" in our home that we need, but let's be honest. All of that stuff usually detracts from the style and mood we are trying to create. We don't need to resign ourselves to a clutter-filled room, closet, or drawer that has become part of life. Discover ways to hide and store some of your most-used items while adding style to your home.

+ Hooks can hold aprons or mugs in the kitchen.

+ A wall-mounted shelf can display your prettiest bowls.

+ An old dresser can be spruced up to hold gloves and scarves in the entry.

A potential clutter hotspot was transformed into a usable guest room closet by providing ample open space for suitcases and personal belongings, and a handy storage chest for extra blankets.

+ Lidded baskets can hold surplus kitchen supplies.

+ A secretary desk could hold dishes, silverware, and placemats.

+ Clear storage drawers can categorize makeup or beauty products.

+ Fabric or metal magazine holders can be used to organize items in a closet.

+ A window box could be hung to hold towels and bathroom necessities.

+ A round-lidded ottoman can store your craft supplies.

+ Desktop mail organizers can hold bills.

+ Muffin tins could hold small accessories in a drawer.

+ A medicine cabinet can be hung for concealed bathroom storage.

+ Glass canisters can be kept on the counter for flour and sugar.

+ A pretty pottery crock can hold extra wooden spoons.

+ Kids' toys can be kept in fabric bins or woven baskets.

+ An old wooden ladder could be hung on the ceiling to hold pots and pans in the kitchen or set against a wall for favorite quilts.

+ Shallow wood boxes can be hung on the wall for glass jars of spices in the kitchen or cosmetics in the bathroom.

+ A coffee table trunk could hide electronics in a family room or keep blankets in a bedroom.

+ Dog food could be kept in lidded metal buckets.

+ Cute flowerpots or jars can hold pens and highlighters on a desk.

+ Favorite teacups or small bowls can hold paperclips or other necessities in drawers.

+ A small cabinet in the dining room could hold glassware.

+ A pretty lidded box could conceal necessities on an open nightstand.

+ A decorative tray can corral jewelry.

+ Fabric-covered containers can hold office supplies, notecards, or mementos.

+ A basket can hold reading material by the bed or a favorite chair.

+ An antique armoire could be repurposed as a clothes closet.

33 | DESIGN "COZY" INTO LARGE ROOMS

Big rooms are wonderful for entertaining, but they aren't always cozy or functional for day-to-day living. Simple ideas will help you and your family fully use and enjoy a large space.

Designate zones. Distinct zones bring intention to a large space. Consider a media or game zone, conversation area, dining area, or a reading nook. Be sure to include a lighting source for a zone.

Divide the space visually. Pillars, ceiling beams, or half walls are permanent division options. Fluid choices include area rugs, a chaise lounge or sofa, wallpaper transitions, large plants, or screens. Paint the ceiling a shade or two darker to divide and cozy up a room.

Anchor areas. Several significant pieces, such as a sectional, large coffee table, built-in bookcase, or a piano, will anchor a room and allow places for smaller pieces to be nestled in and not lost.

Increase the scale. Opt for proportionate, taller furniture, especially if you have vaulted ceilings. Consider a large bookcase, an armoire, and chairs and sofas with tall backs.

Double up. Center a conversation area with two matching square ottomans in the center. Use two area rugs to shape two different zones. Double up with a pair of chairs, two matching large lamps, etc.

Avoid wall hugging. Bring furniture in around a focal point, such as a fireplace. Save wall space for art, buffets, consoles, shelving, or additional conversation areas.

Go bigger. Up your game and choose bigger, bolder art and accessories. Go with extra big frames and/or add larger matting to showcase art and photos. Consider a vibrant, large-image painting.

Connect with texture. If your room feels cold or cavernous, bring in additional layers of curtain panels, throw blankets, rugs, and upholstered pieces. Repeated patterns or colors will unite the space.

34 | STREAMLINE SMALL SPACES

Make room for what you love. Pare down or consolidate items. What could you get rid of? What can you store out of sight to eliminate clutter? Limit your number of storage options too.

Look up. Draw the line of sight upward with tall mirrors and furniture, a wall gallery, painted vertical stripes, striped curtains, or drapes hung above the window frame.

Be intentional. Conceal clutter in small spaces. Establish order in an entry area with a memo board, a dresser, and a key rack. Create an office nook with a work station on casters or a laptop in a secretary hutch. Add hooks for storage and wall shelves for visual displays.

Build it in. Consider a built-in bookcase or storage window seat to ease visual clutter. Free-standing units nestled into a corner or against a wall offer similar benefits.

Get grounded. In an awkwardly shaped room, a horizontal-striped rug can help visually center and widen your space. A statement light fixture can bring clarity and style to an uninspired room.

Choose functional furniture. The right pieces can make all the difference:

+ tall and narrow shelving

+ round ottomans or coffee tables

+ nesting tables

+ small scale and armless pieces

+ drop-leaf dining tables, desk stations, or side tables

+ corner storage pieces

+ storage containers that fit under beds or couches

+ mirrors to expand visual space

+ dual-function selections (a dining room cabinet that offers space for dish storage and a surface for serving)

Bring in the benches. Benches are one of the most versatile pieces for any home. Use them for storage, seating, shelving, tables, foot stools, and zone dividers.

35 | EMBELLISH YOUR FURNITURE

Don't buy something new when you can refresh what you have. Give what you have some love. Enjoy the process and result of trying something different!

+ Dab metallic paint on handles or other hardware for a new look.

+ Paper the interior of an open bookcase with gift wrap, maps, wall paper, or ornate scrapbook paper.

+ Drape fabric over a lackluster chair as a slipcover. Look at drapes, sheets, and bolts of fabric as potential material for this furniture refresh! (A soft drop cloth can even be fashioned as a slipcover to conceal a dated upholstered ottoman.)

Give what you have some love.

Touchable
TEXTURES

Touchable
TEXTURES

Your favorite destinations are filled with an interesting mix of textures. Texture is everywhere in nature! Imagine the tactile experience of a walk on the beach. You feel the warm grains of sand beneath your feet and the contrast of the cool glassy tide pools. You notice the texture of the foam that bubbles on the waves and the white fluffy clouds floating effortlessly across the clear blue sky. The mix of jagged rocks and smooth driftwood are a significant part of the experience.

Just as the combination of organic elements is foundational to our sense of enjoyment and pleasure in nature, they are essential to our delight in our home. If you sense something is missing in your own space, you might only need to create more complex layers of tactile and visual texture.

To establish an inviting experience, each room in your home should include a variety of touchable materials, accessories, and points of interest. Incorporating a carefully chosen mix of textures will delight your eyes as well as bring comfort to the space.

Each piece plays a significant part in the overall look and feel of your home. The hardware you love, the fabrics you select, the furniture and useful items within help create an experience. How you arrange the elements and combine the functional and decorative pieces in your space builds layers of texture and contrast.

While it might seem complicated to create a space with many layers, you don't have to be a professional to pull together a well-designed room. There are many easy ways and simple guidelines to add depth to your style and touchable texture to your home.

36 | INTRODUCE TEXTURE WITH INTENTION

Add texture with intention by incorporating a variety of materials into your floor and wall treatments, furniture, lighting, decorative accessories, and fabrics. The options are endless!

wood	stone	linen	corduroy	canvas
rattan	mirror	leather	cable knit	crewel
paint	metal	suede	flannel	lace
acrylic	ceramic	silk	fleece	jute
lacquer	crystal	velvet	wool	beads
glass	pottery	faux fur	chenille	cork
marble	tweed	cashmere	chambray	concrete

37 | TRANSFORM A SPACE WITH PILLOWS AND THROWS

Changing and adding pillows is one of the most versatile ways to refresh a room. Not only do they provide comfort and a finishing touch, they can add pizazz to an otherwise blah space or tone down a busy room. The right mix of shapes, sizes, colors, and patterns can bring your look together with your unique flair.

+ Select pillows that are appropriately sized and shaped both visually and functionally for your space. Accent pillows should not be too small. A 20" pillow works for most sofas.

+ Oblong or round pillows are great accent pillows at the center of a sofa, bed or on chairs.

+ For an extra plush look, invest in down or down-blend pillows. Down lasts far longer than foam inserts and has a softer look.

+ To stretch your seasonal design options, use removable pillow covers. For the fullest look, use a down-blend insert one size bigger than your cover.

+ Vary the scale of your pillow patterns so the overall effect in the room is pleasing.

+ Solid pillows can tone down a room full of pattern as well as help define a cohesive palette.

+ Select a unified color scheme for all of the pillows in a room.

+ If you mix pillow patterns, select one hue that will be your common denominator.

+ Select prints with tone-on-tone or neutral colors for a less busy look.

+ Odd numbers of pillows and symmetrical placement on a sofa are visually pleasing.

+ If you use only two pillows on a sofa, choose one solid and one patterned for visual interest.

+ Add in pillows with texture too! Think about fur, knit, and silky options for a fun mix.

+ Arrange your pillows with a 2-2-1 formula. Two matching, equally sized and shaped pillows on either end of a sofa; two smaller, like-sized pillows in a different fabric next to them; and one smaller accent pillow in the middle. Try one of these coordinating combinations:

Outer pillows: matching, polka-dot patterned 22"-26" square pillows

Next: matching, floral 20" square pillows

Middle: one solid 12" x 20"

Outer pillows: matching, solid 20" square pillows

Next: matching, striped, or plaid 20" square pillows in coordinating colors

Middle: one large-scale floral 12" x 20" pillow

+ Try a 2-1 combination for smaller couches or love seats.

38 | BALANCE WITH CONTRAST

What stands out as your dominant textures and tones? Add in whatever contrasting textures will provide balance. Surprisingly, contrast can be the key to a welcoming harmony in a room.

+ Complement a room of primarily painted furniture pieces with those that are natural wood or glass and vice versa.

+ Enhance a room that has a lot of fabric and softness with a basket, large shell, collection of stones, or a natural fiber rug.

+ Get creative with different pairings to see what you enjoy.

+ Brighten a dark room with light-colored furniture or accessories.

+ Place lamps where they will provide ambient light to soften starkness or shadows and clear the black holes.

+ Balance neutrals with color and off-set a colorful room with neutrals.

+ Contrast the smooth sheen of silverware and ceramic plates with table runners, place mats, and napkins in natural and textured materials.

+ Bring in plants, such as a potted fern, bouquet of flowers, or a gathering of potted succulents, to provide texture and life to a furnished space.

CREATIVE CONTRASTS

solid, sleek items with pieces that have a patina

sheens with matted finishes and fibrous textures

woven blankets with soft fleece or silky choices

natural elements with decor bling (chandeliers, shiny metal accessories and hardware, colored glass, or metal furniture trim)

BY WISDOM A HOUSE
IS BUILT AND THROUGH
UNDERSTANDING IT IS
ESTABLISHED;
THROUGH KNOWLEDGE
ITS ROOMS ARE FILLED
WITH RARE AND
BEAUTIFUL TREASURE
PROVERBS 24:3

39 | PLAY WITH PATTERNS

A mix of patterns can make a room feel vibrant and welcoming. Here are some secrets for successful pattern mixing!

Decide the mood. If you want a lively space, a mix of colors and patterns bring energy to a room. If you crave calm, choose subtle patterns or tone-on-tone, textured elements.

Anchor with neutrals. A solid rug, neutral-fabric ottoman, or a simplified paint palette will balance lively elements. If you have patterned furniture, use neutrals to create a new foundation for those existing patterns.

Plan your pattern palette. Select a couple of colors (for instance, shades of blue and white or a mix of green, blue, and white) and stick to that limited color scheme as you add patterned items. Pare away existing patterns that don't work with the new plan.

Start with a formula. Mix patterns with confidence by using a simple guideline:

> a solid + a small scale + a large scale

For example, if you choose shades of blue, gray, and white, start with a solid light blue pillow. Next, add a small-scale pattern in navy blue and white (such as a tiny polka-dot print). Then add a large-scale light blue, white, and dark gray pillow (perhaps a floral).

Experiment for fun. Once you've mastered the basics, mix in additional colors and several scales of patterns.

Visualize the whole picture. Evaluate all the patterns in a room as a whole. Do they work together? Note elements that will read as a pattern, such as flooring materials (textured or patterned wood, rugs, or tile), furnishings (notice lines or intricate shapes), light fixtures, wall coverings, cabinets, counters, and ceilings.

Take pictures of your patterns. Refer to these photos when considering a purchase to complement your look. Or photograph items at the store to evaluate at home.

40 | LEAN OBJECTS FOR EASE AND BEAUTY

Leaning a few objects against walls or other backdrops creates visual texture. I started to lean items when a previous home had plaster too fragile to support hanging items. I loved the effect so much that, to this day, it's one of my favorite decor tips.

WHY?

+ easy to change up

+ hides unsightly items, such as outlets, vents, and plaster or flooring flaws

+ more dimension, variance, interest, and casual charm

+ more angle options than hanging allows

WHAT?

+ framed artwork or photos

+ canvassed pieces, such as lettered art

+ architectural pieces, such as shutters

+ mirrors

+ metal or wood signs

+ stained glass panels

+ antique washboards

+ intricate iron wall art

+ vintage doors, window frames, ladders

+ chalkboard panels

+ smaller accessories, photos, or paintings next to larger pieces

WHERE?

+ back of bookshelves

+ tabletops

+ mantels

+ windowsills

+ floors

+ stair landings

HOW?

- + Bigger, heavier architectural pieces or mirrors can lean by themselves without additional layers, while smaller artwork usually looks best with multiple pieces layered and overlapped.

- + Place shorter accessories or stacked books in front of a taller leaning or background piece.

- + Stabilize smaller pieces with sticky tack to keep them from slipping and sliding.

- + Secure larger elements for safety with a picture hook or Command Strips (Velcro hangers).

- + When leaning mirrors, always check to see what you are reflecting in them.

41 | LAYER YOUR LINENS

Pamper yourself with the warmth and texture of layered bedding. A mix of fabrics creates a visually luxurious style and a refreshing sleep experience each night. Here are three layers for a cozy and textured bed.

1. Comfortable Sheets. When you can, invest in comfortable, high-quality, higher-thread-count sheets. You can choose simple white or a solid color and add pattern and texture with other bedding or try the reverse. Use solids and textures on the top layers and have the patterns surprise you when you pull back the covers! Try sheets in fun stripes, florals, or polka dots.

2. Mix of Blankets. For visual interest and comfort flexibility, layer a blanket and then a lightweight quilt over the sheets. For extra coziness, add an additional fluffy duvet or throw blanket loosely folded or draped at the end of the bed.

3. Plenty of Pillows. Layers of pillows will add height and dimension to your bed. For a stylishly layered queen bed, select a combination of at least two Euro-style pillows (big square pillows), two standard pillows with shams, and a center accent pillow. For a playful look, mix patterned or colored shams. Create the feel you love with different pillow fabric textures: grain sack, faux fur, knit covers, or pillows with a surprising metallic sheen.

42 | WARM UP WITH WOOD

A single element can transform a space. Wood will add texture, beauty, and visual interest. Here are some ways to warm up your room.

ACCESSORIES

Enhance your kitchen with wood cutting boards, wood spoons, and wood bowls. Add subtle touches to other rooms with crates and woven baskets, and frames and wood sculptures.

FLOORS, WALLS, AND WINDOW

Warmth and texture added to your beautiful backdrops, from floor to ceiling, will make your home cozy: bamboo, woven rugs; wood paneling and molding; blinds, curtain rods, and finials. We used a tree branch as a curtain rod in my son's former room for a rustic touch.

FURNITURE

Any room can be warmed up with one piece of wood furniture. Consider a table or chair for a gathering area, an island for your kitchen, a headboard for the bedroom, and a wood storage element in your bathroom.

How do you want to warm up your style?

Artful
ACCESSORIES

Artful
ACCESSORIES

People who collect treasures as they experience life adventures can create such personal and welcoming homes! The most interesting rooms will tell the most fascinating tales. Your story is uniquely yours to tell, whether you have traveled the world or made a home in one place. The practical elements you use every day and the accessories you gather over time should reflect your personal history, taste, and passions.

Your style should be ever evolving as you grow and your taste is refined. Don't rush the process! Your home should not be a static snapshot of the person you were at one point in time. Enjoy the adventure of continually refreshing your space as you collect, display, and arrange accessories and functional elements that speak to you so they can breathe new life and soul into your home.

43 | MAKE A STATEMENT

Knickknacks might catch our eye when we are shopping, but little odds and ends can feel lost in a larger room. Too many pieces spread out on every surface will make a room feel more cluttered than decorated. To unify your space, start with a clean slate. Remove the accessories from each surface. Replace accessories by adopting the "less is more" principle. How could you make bolder design statements with fewer pieces? Train your eye to carefully edit what you display in a room and then make a statement with a standout piece or two:

+ a large ceramic container on an entry table

+ a large pair of candlesticks on a mantel

+ an oversized light in your dining area

+ a substantial potted plant in a corner

+ a large mirror in your living room

+ a large scale art canvas

Smaller pieces can still find a home. Arrange similar items together on a tray or area of a surface for more visibility. Groupings of frames, figurines, books, or dishes can be presented as a collection for a bigger impact.

44 | BEAUTIFY REAL LIFE

Those everyday items you and your family reach for throughout the day can be your most important, most artful accessories. When you choose functional pieces that are beautiful, your home will be well decorated and tell your story even without decorative tchotchkes. Select practical items in styles, colors, and patterns that inspire you. Coordinate collections of everyday necessities and display them creatively so they will contribute to your overall look. Keep your decorative elements simple and focus on making real life beautiful.

EVERYDAY ON DISPLAY

dishes	hooks
pitchers	candlesticks and holders
colorful mugs and teacups	tote bags
kitchenware	umbrella stands
plates	mirrors
serving trays	jewelry boxes
chalkboards	wooden game boards
books and bookends	heirlooms or family hand-me-downs
baskets	quilts

45 | COLLECT 7 SIMPLE DECOR ACCESSORIES

The look and feel of your home will develop over time. Along the way, choose a few favorite accessories to collect. These 7 decor items are easy to find and simple to add to any room's look.

1. Plates and Platters. Collect pretty plates in your favorite colors and patterns for your table and your walls! To save space, use white plates and platters for everyday use and mix in specialty items.

2. Metal Pieces. Hang attractive pots and pans on racks or stack them for display on shelves.

3. Throw Blankets. Gather quilts or blankets of varying textures and colors to drape over a chair or fold and stack on a shelf as a decorative element.

4. Artwork. Collect art to commemorate significant events, such as anniversaries and special family moments. Look for prints, postcards, greetings cards, maps, or books.

5. Vases and Vessels. Whether you fill them with objects or leave them empty, special vases and vessels are statement accents for shelves, mantels, or entryway surfaces.

6. Baskets. Handmade woven baskets can be useful to carry or corral wayward pieces or to create a home for less attractive items. Even hang them on your wall as unexpected art!

7. Books. Vintage or collectible books add personality and texture to tabletops or shelving to elevate other special items on surfaces, making a house feel like a lived-in home.

46 | GO ON A TREASURE HUNT

Swap accessories between rooms for immediate, no-cost makeovers. When you are ready to refresh a space, take a look through your cabinets, closets, other rooms, and yard for cool stuff to use in a new way. Just because an item has sat in the same spot for years doesn't mean it has to stay put. You'll never know what will work until you try it! You might be surprised how much more you'll love your space if you simply move accessories around. Try these unexpected pieces in a new location:

a twisty branch	an old gate or window frame
table runners	a collection of postcards
a wood or glass box	musical instruments
pretty scarves	lamps or lampshades

47 | DIY: CREATE SENTIMENTAL ART

We all have little treasures that spark special memories, but how often do those items see the light of day? Usually they are stuffed in boxes, out of sight. Make your memories a part of your life. Create sentimental art to use as a statement piece or as a focal point for a gallery wall.

For this DIY, select items that are from meaningful people or moments: the blouse you wore when your husband proposed, your daughter's newborn hat, your grandma's doilies, an uncle's plaid shirt, your mom's wedding gloves, or a favorite piece of jewelry that you don't wear anymore.

1. Gather the meaningful pieces you want to display as art.

2. Find a linen place mat or piece of wrapping paper to be the backdrop.

3. Affix the backdrop to the back of the frame or to a piece of sturdy foam board with fabric glue.

4. Tack the memento to the backing, use fabric glue, decorative pushpins, or inconspicuous staples.

5. Frame the art, or use bull clips or even clipboards to showcase your art! Leave off the glass if your art is dimensional.

6. Hang this new art in a geometric grid or a free flowing gallery wall or just highlight one or two special pieces together.

48 | DISPLAY WITH DIMENSION

A few simple tips will help you add style and character to your displays.

Design high to low and front to back. A display will usually look best when you use accessories in different heights, decorating high to low or layering against a wall or shelf front to back. Tall items can be vases, a leaning frame, a willow branch in a glass jug, or a cluster of smaller items on top of a stack of books or plates. Then mix in the lower accessories for a visually interesting effect.

Vary the impact. Add round items to soften straight lines, include various thicknesses and sizes, pair opposite textures, include an organic element, and mix in the unexpected.

Create a focal point. A mirror or piece of framed artwork hung above a mantel or a shelving unit automatically creates an interesting focal point *and* a backdrop for the accessories you place on that surface.

49 | DECORATE WITH NATURAL ELEMENTS

Including nature in your home's decor is one of the easiest, least expensive, and most attractive ways to blend any season with your style.

FLOWERS IN UNIQUE CONTAINERS

Place your blooms in a coffee tin, galvanized bucket, soup tureen, pitcher, antique toolbox, or a decorative bowl.

DRIFTWOOD, BRANCHES, OR ANTLERS

Try leaning a tall branch in a corner. Use a piece of driftwood as a simple centerpiece or even as an organic curtain rod. Add antlers to a gallery wall for a three dimensional, natural element.

MIXED ELEMENTS

Fill glass lamps or vases with pinecones, cinnamon sticks, shells, sand, moss, and ornaments during the holidays.

NATURAL TONES AND TEXTURES

Decorate with nature's colors and materials. Consider leather, rattan, and wood. Mixing and matching neutral shades and items will unite your look.

COASTAL INSPIRATIONS

If you love the beach the way I do, incorporate coastal elements in your decor. Use subtle colors of the sea, starfish, shell bowls, or artwork depicting ocean scenes.

SIMPLE GREENERY

Place a plant clipping from your yard in a glass jug or jar. Air plants are an easy option and virtually impossible to kill (a win-win). Plant succulents in a teacup collection for a pretty touch.

NATURAL CENTERPIECES

Fill a tray, bowl, or wreath with pebbles and candles. Border with fruit, moss, pinecones, etc. Cover a cake stand surface with these elements for a visual feast.

50 | FILL YOUR HOME WITH GRATITUDE

There are many ways to decorate your home. Each effort you make to improve your surroundings is a valuable one, but don't let unfinished projects or an unfulfilled wish list lessen the joy of having a place that embraces you, your family, and the guests who come and go. Make the time to enjoy and fully live in the spaces you create, filling your home with not only material possessions, but with a sense of gratitude for what you already have.

It's a haven.

It's a place for rest.

It's an expression of you.

It's an invitation to others.

It's a gift.

YOUR INVITATION
TO INSPIRATION

MAKE YOUR HOME A
SANCTUARY—NOT A SHOWPLACE

Welcome to *The Inspired Room*. Forget about the rules and discover inspired ways to personalize your spaces and express your style with texture, color, and your favorite treasures. Room by room, you'll shape a home that is inspired by the people, beauty, and life you love.

Step inside Melissa's home as she shares lessons learned, inspiring photos, and encouraging insights to help you embrace your authentic style.

COLOR YOUR WAY TO INSPIRATION

This is your creative opportunity to relax and unwind. More than just an invitation to color, *The Inspired Room Coloring Book* encourages you to be inspired as you design the home of your dreams.

You'll find inspiration for every room in your home as you have fun experimenting with color palettes, playing with fun patterns, imagining the possibilities through creative activities, and coloring beautiful pages that bring your dreams to life.

TAKE BACK YOUR SPACE
AND LOVE YOUR HOME AGAIN

CREATE THE HOME OF YOUR DREAMS RIGHT WHERE YOU ARE

You can love your home again. Join Melissa as she helps you look past the tiny flaws, every-day messes, and the mix of hand-me-down furniture and focus on what truly matters—how your home shapes your life, relationships, and dreams.

Dare to see your surroundings with new eyes that just might inspire a change of heart. And get ready to *Love the Home You Have*.

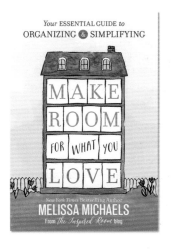

CLEAR OUT THE CLUTTER AND MAKE ROOM FOR WHAT MATTERS

If all the stuff you have is starting to take over your home and life, let Melissa offer insightful ideas for altering your habits while efficiently decluttering and organizing you home so you can really enjoy living there.

With a little encouragement and practical advice, you will be inspired to create a place for the things you love and breathing room to pursue your dreams and engage in life with the people who matter most.

About the
AUTHOR

Melissa Michaels is the creator and author of the popular home decorating blog *The Inspired Room*, which inspires women to love the home they have. Since 2007 Melissa has been encouraging hundreds of thousands of readers a month with daily posts and inspiration for all things house and home. *The Inspired Room* was twice voted as the *Better Homes and Gardens* magazine Reader's Choice decorating blog.

Melissa lives with her husband, Jerry; their son, Luke; and two impossibly adorable Doodle pups, Jack and Lily, whose adventures are well loved and followed on their Facebook page (Facebook.com/jack.goldendoodle). The Michaels' daughters, Courtney and Kylee (and Kylee's husband, Lance), are an active part of *The Inspired Room*.

CONNECT WITH MELISSA AND OTHER HOME LOVERS

The Inspired Room Blog - **theinspiredroom.net**

Subscribe - Have new blog posts delivered to your inbox.

melissa@theinspiredroom.com.

Facebook.com/**theinspiredroom.fans**

Instagram

Pinterest — **@theinspiredroom**

Twitter